The South Side

of the Haystack

CONTENTS

ACKNOWLDEGEMENTS

Credit for the memories expressed in these writings is shared by several people.

Most importantly it belongs to my parents who provided the safe and caring environment in which I was allowed to express my creativity. They must have shaken their heads many times at the strange and varied ways I chose to do that. If they were still here to read this I think it would have brought smiles to their faces.

It also belongs to my brothers and sisters who added flavor and excitement to my life on a daily basis. Although they may recall events or details differently, I hope that the narratives initiate a positive journey down memory lane for them.

No lesser part is shared by the people who lived in that small farming community. Our neighbors, my teachers, my fellow students and the church parishioners all enriched my childhood experiences.

While trying to capture these memories I am indebted to several people for the application of their expertise.

- To Joanne who was able to turn the key that set the reflections in motion. Thank you for sharing your amazing gift.

- To my friend Audrey, who encouraged me to begin writing and critiqued my early efforts.

- To my friend and colleague, Fay Jorgenson, for her editorial reviews.

- To my daughter, Sandy, for her artistic layout critique.

- But mostly to my wife, Karen, who provided encouragement, suggestions, proof-reading proficiency, and the freedom to write when the stories were ready to emerge. In addition, her many artistic representations so vividly brought my childhood recollections to life.

When first my way to fair I took
Few pence in purse had I,
And long I used to stand and look
At things I could not buy.

Now times are altered; if I care
To buy a thing, I can;
The pence are here and here's the fair,
But where is that young man?

...A. E. Houseman

The 1950s were a heady time. The economy was on an upswing. New ways of doing things were constantly being invented. The standard of living was improving at an unprecedented rate. All of these factors influenced the family farm as well. Power had come to rural areas and along with it indoor plumbing, furnaces and freezers. The combine allowed one person to do the work of dozens. Everywhere enterprising farmers embraced and applied the new technologies.

Except on the farm where I grew up.

My parents and their seven children had just emigrated from Europe where wartime politics had divested them of a prosperous farming operation for the second time in their lives. Having to abandon all their belongings and property left them with only the generosity of family and strangers to rely on. Through the efforts of my grandmother and my father's siblings, who had come to this country twenty years earlier, a farm property, located near the hamlet of Spondin, approximately half way between Hanna and Coronation, was secured with a minimal down payment.

To this strange land and into a completely unfamiliar agricultural environment, my parents brought the only tools that they had available to them... physical strength and determination. Together with the generosity and frequent assistance of family and neighbors, they began farming in the only way they knew. With these assets they achieved what many pioneers of earlier years had... they raised a family of resourceful, productive children who all have contributed in positive ways to this country that embraced them.

While accomplishing this not inconsequential task, they also paid all their bills, saved for their retirement and contributed some of these scarce resources to those less fortunate, thus leaving a legacy that anyone could be proud of.

While our neighbors embraced the new farming technology, we did a lot of our work with horses. Tractors did not appear until later and even when they did, horses were still employed for many tasks. Loose haystacks occupied our winter feeding area while the neighbors had stacks of bales in theirs. During harvest time ours was the only binder and threshing machine to be seen on the fields as the other farmers had long since changed to swathers and combines.

Equally primitive were our household living conditions. Indoor plumbing never did come to our farmhouse. Central heating remained the job of the kitchen stove by means of the wood and coal that fueled it. Although electricity came to many of the neighboring farms, it did not come to ours until much later because of cost and the lack of foreseeable applications. Consequently all of our evening light was supplied by one coal oil lamp set on the kitchen table. Sitting in my bedroom and reading by the light of that lamp in the other room was a common occurrence.

While we had a fence wire telephone that worked once or twice during the years we lived there, most of the time the nearest functioning telephone was four miles away at the general store and it would be accessed only in times of emergency.

Thus it seemed that our operation was at least a generation behind in its methods and conveniences and this proved to be a constant source of consternation for a young lad with 'modern' ideas and desires.

However, backward reflection puts a different light on that whole situation. The generational lag provided the opportunity to experience things that my peers only heard about from their parents during the "when I was young" discourses. Therefore, had my parents been cutting-edge leaders in their everyday lives, the following vignettes could not have been written from experience and I now realize that my life would have been the poorer for it.

The South Side
of the Haystack

Preparing for winter occupied most of the summer's work program and laying winter feed in store for the farm animals was a major part of that activity. "Making hay while the sun shines" was an apt descriptor of this activity since it took place during the hottest part of the year, usually the entire month of July.

Because of mosquitoes and the unforgiving hay dust and hay spears, a scantily clad body was not an option. If anything, clothing was increased in thickness so that the effects of these annoying elements would be minimized. This made the culinary term "stewing in its own juices" a very accurate description.

Haying involved several stages, each depending on the proper completion of the preceding one. A team of horses was hitched to a mower and during the succeeding circuits of the field the grass gradually succumbed to the supremacy of the sickle blades. A rake became the next horse-drawn implement in the process. With this the fallen grass was carefully gathered into rows and then

small piles. Finally the team was called upon to pull a hayrack alongside the piles while we pitched the hay onto it with forks until it could hold no more.

The rack would be pulled to the storage site, usually near the winter feeding spots. At this location the hay would be placed in a neat pile of a certain size and shape. This pile then had to be "finished" so as to shed the fall and winter moisture in the most efficient manner. In our family this "finishing" was done by the expert... my mother.

When the stack was near its completion, she would climb to its top and receive the last layer as it was tossed up to her. Each forkful was placed into position with great care being taken to layer it just so. That being done to her satisfaction, she would accept a series of weights, tied together with left over binder twine, which she would drape over the stack in several places. Now neither wind nor rain nor any other form of weather would disturb this masterpiece until it was used during the winter feeding time.

It was hard work and probably one of the least liked activities of any season, but in spite of that there were some positive benefits. Cold water tasted better during those days. The lunch break was ever so sweet, if too short. Cholesterol and extra body fat were of no concern when one labored from dawn until dusk.

But the unsurpassed benefit of this activity came six to eight months later when the temperature dipped far below zero and the wind shrieked out of the north. It was then that on a sunny afternoon I could bundle up and head for the south side of the haystack. There I could snuggle in to the loose stack of piled-up hay and soak up the rays. It had to be a sample of what heaven was like, I thought.

Today I stood on the south side of my house, basking in its shelter and enjoying the warm sunshine. I thought of those old-fashioned times and I missed them.

Birds
of a Feather

With a hiss of steam and a shriek of brakes, the massive beast wheezed up to the staging area where several shadowy figures waited silently in the encroaching darkness. A lone man emerged from the locomotive, pulled open a large doorway and began unloading one box after another, stacking them carefully on the platform near the waiting observers.

It was an anticipated rendezvous and a shiver of excitement ran through me as I watched the proceedings. One of the boxes emitted small chirping sounds and the quiet group of people slowly approached it. Yes, the label identified it as belonging to us and after arranging for the appropriate release forms the container was gently lifted onto the back of our truck and we were on our way home with this spring's supply of little chicks.

The outdoor chicken coop remained dark and silent on this night since this cargo was still far too precious to consign to a home that far away from my mother's observant eye. Since their arrival had not been unexpected, a loving homecoming had been arranged for them. Around the back and one side of the kitchen stove a row of boxes marked the border of what was to be an impromptu chicken pen for the next week or two. Newspapers had been carefully placed on the floor inside

this enclosure, with water and food containers positioned in key locations.

Into this warm, welcoming environment the little balls of fluff disembarked and joined our family. For the next while we became accustomed to being awakened by the chirping of hungry mouths and lulled to sleep by the peeps from mounds of huddled hatchlings as they settled in for the night.

These first few days were critical to the survival of the newcomers. Food and water had to be carefully regulated. Newspaper bedding had to be replaced daily. Mounds of chicks had to be disturbed frequently to ensure that none succumbed to suffocation from their attempts to embrace each other's warmth.

As I watched them frolicking during this adorable stage I did not comprehend that their contribution to our lives would cost them theirs. I did not think about the source of the tasty fried chicken that my mother often prepared. It was to be an introduction to the interdependence of all creatures and to the cycle of life through which we all pass.

Although a tasty bite was the eventual destination of these birds, until that time they contributed much to the economy of our mixed farming operation. As they grew older many of them produced eggs that were collected daily and used for food or stored until a large crateful could be shipped to market.

21

Since these eggs provided the grocery money that was needed to supplement what could not be produced on our farm, the collection process was deemed one of the most important in the daily routine.

It was also one of the most dangerous chores undertaken.

Leading huge horses to water or dodging the wicked kicks of cows reluctant to be milked was child's play compared to facing a hen that did not appreciate being deprived of her hard won trophies. The anticipated jab of her hard beak as I reached under her warm body to retrieve these forced donations created a great deal of anxiety that I'm sure stunted my growth considerably. It must have been the fear of appearing unequal to the task that spurred me on to meet this daily challenge, as nothing else explains why I would continually subject myself to this punishment.

As if the recalcitrant hens were not enough of a problem, an even greater obstacle was the ever watchful guardian of the flock, the rooster. While the hens would only object when I reached for the egg, this two-legged defender was much more aggressive in his tactics and did not wait for me to get close to the nests. Recognizing my approach as a threat, he would fly at my face at the earliest opportunity. His cocky attitude certainly took the fun out of this task.

Gradually though, one by one, our feathered companions succumbed to the call of the frying pan and made their final contribution. During one fall day the remaining members of the group were gathered up and all dispatched at once to be preserved for consumption during the long, cold winter.

Not all of them gave up without one last bid for freedom, however. While my mother performed the killing, it was my father's job to hold the dead bird while it bled out and also to hand the next live bird to her. In the interests of efficiency he would use one hand for each task. This efficiency led to a rare burst of laughter as he forgot which hand held which bird, and lay down a live one by mistake. A look of complete astonishment came over his face as this 'dead' bird got up and walked away.

It was then time to be reminded of that tasty fried chicken because that was the only way I could force myself to endure the unpleasant chicken plucking job which followed. As boiling water was poured over the feathers they surrendered all of the putrid odors that they had collected throughout the season directly into my hesitant nostrils.

There was no need to encourage me to make this task of as short duration as possible, although it seemed to take forever to cleanse one bird to my mother's inspection standards. Thankfully my father could pluck several chickens for every one that I finished, thus hastening the completion of this unpleasant stage of the process.

I open a barrel of KFC and dig out a drumstick, biting into it with gusto. Although the eleven different herbs and spices do their best to ensure a satisfactory gastronomic experience, it isn't enough to equal the satisfaction I used to get from a similar meal many years ago. But then I think of the hen, the rooster and the feathers and I close my eyes and silently thank the Colonel.

Trouble
Is My Name!

Getting into trouble can be an invigorating learning experience. It brings an adrenaline rush of excitement that is hard to get any other way. I think that's why we do it so effortlessly. Put the possibility of trouble in front of us and we will eventually choose to explore it just to see what will happen.

I'm sure that I got into trouble a lot more often than I remember. I was likely instrumental in getting other people into trouble just as often.

The Carriage Miscarriage

One of the first such incidents is one that I actually have no recollection of, but have been told about often enough so that it almost seems that I do.

One fine spring day it was the job of two of my older siblings to take me for a walk in the fresh air. It would be more accurate to say that they went for a walk whereas I rode in style… in a baby carriage.

The sun shone brightly from a clear blue sky and a warm breeze softly stirred the newly emerging foliage as my caregivers and I ventured down the lane. Since their instructions were to keep me entertained in this manner for as long as possible, their wanderings took us ever further and eventually to the top of a rise with gentle slopes on either side. Had I been looking in the right direction I likely would have noticed the light bulb appearing over one of their heads as the perfect idea landed.

"Let's notch the entertainment value of this experience up a level," might have been the words that expressed this bright idea. "I'm certain that our little brother would really enjoy traveling at a greater rate of speed, don't you think?" Instant agreement immediately put the plan into motion.

Now to be fair, some plans regarding necessary safety measures did precede this adventure, since one of them went to the bottom of the grade first to await my arrival. The part that wasn't adequately considered was how the steering could be controlled once the carriage was on its own. In any case, since remote-controlled vehicles had yet to be invented my caregivers were somewhat limited in their options.

Down the gentle slope went my coach carrying its gleeful passenger at an ever increasing, but still moderate speed. What a thrill that must have been!

Besides the steering, another slight flaw in the planning process became evident. They had entirely forgotten to scout out the location of the activity in advance. Spring, you see, was also the time for a thorough cleaning of all farm buildings, including the barn and animal pens. Because of the current environmental management practices, the gathered remains of this animal refuse were piled up to await its gradual composting at which time it could be used to feed newly planted garden shoots.

These two lapses in the planning, the failure to scout out the location and the inability to control the steering, resulted in an unanticipated yet very soft landing as the carriage careened off the desired path and came to a gentle stop at the manure pile, depositing its precious cargo directly into it.

I wish that I could remember the explanation that was offered to my mother upon our return to the house. For some reason, I was never told about that part of the story.

The Cream of the Crop

Having been successful at my first known attempt to get into or create trouble, it seemed only appropriate that it be tried again. You'd think my mother would have known better by now, but perhaps she thought the punishment that had been meted out following the carriage experience would certainly preclude any more such lapses in judgment. Once again, I was made the responsibility of an older sibling, but what my mother hadn't counted on was that this time I was old enough to apply my own lapse of judgment.

While visiting with my cousins, a game of hide and seek was chosen to allow all ages to participate in a meaningful way. I pondered for a time where I might conceal my small frame most effectively. And then I had it! Who would ever think of looking for me in the 'ice house', the outdoor refrigerator of the day?

As with a modern refrigerator, the ice house was used to keep perishable items from spoiling quickly. What was missing in those days was a Tupperware lid that could be counted upon to make a good seal that would prevent spillage or in this case "steppage".

In my eagerness to escape my perfect hiding place and make my 'home free' declaration to my pursuer, I inadvertently stepped with my dirty shoe into a full container of fresh farm cream.

There are some problems that became instantly evident.

Firstly, cream was a valuable commodity requiring several steps of manual labor to produce. It also required several days of collection in order to provide sufficient quantities to take to market and to be used in artistic kitchen creations.

Secondly the cream did not belong to my family, thus making the offense even graver.

However, a four-year old still fit under the provisions of my aunt's version of the Young Offenders Act, and therefore, could not really be held accountable or punished.

So in order to continue the illusion that she was still in control of her offspring, my mother chose the only action that seemed reasonable. She blamed my carelessness on my older sister's lack of supervision.

Wildlife Unlimited

Long before I knew what wildlife conservationists were, my father valued and applied similar fundamental principles. While gophers and sparrows were fair game for hunting ventures, most other wildlife was off limits. Ducks and geese were safe on our sloughs as they journeyed north and south. Killdeers, meadow larks, red-winged blackbirds, barn swallows, and other such wildlife could exist without fear of being caught in the crosshairs of a rifle.

One instance taught this lesson to me in a way that I never forgot. It was the time of new life arising from the earth and springing from the wombs of the many animals in our care.

My father and brother were loading straw to be used as bedding for the cows and their new-born calves. This straw stack was one of many that was situated out in the fields where the crop had been threshed in the fall.

Being too young to help with this chore afforded my little sister and me the luxury of using the time to explore the straw stack environment. It appeared that cows and calves were not the only ones who thought this to be good nest making material. There in one corner of the stack, nicely hidden from plain view was a nest of duck eggs.

If 'two heads are better than one', then two children egging each other on was surely a recipe for trouble. We must have decided it would be good fun to break these eggs either because we could, or because we wanted to see if they looked like the chicken eggs that we often saw gathered and used for various food preparations. To our amazement, inside all of them were the partially formed bodies of baby ducklings, quite a wonder to behold!

When the rack was fully loaded, my father came to find us so that we could travel home. I never saw his anger very often, but on that occasion there was no doubt about his feelings. 'Wildlife like this was to be respected and allowed to prosper' was the lesson taught to us in a multi-media presentation that day. The words were clear. Even clearer was the old-fashioned 'lickin' that accompanied them.

The Long Arm of the Law

One would think that if I could stay out of trouble anywhere, it would have been in church, but I found a way to experience it there also.

It was the custom in our church for everyone to stand during prayer time. As a youngster one of my missions in life was to be just as cool as my peers and for them, lounging, not standing was a preferred posture. One Sunday I bravely decided I would venture that pose also.

When all stood for the prayer, I leaned over and put my elbows on the back of the bench in front of me, thus striking the casual stance that I knew would impress my friends. Before I could bask in the glory of their adulation, there came a sharp jab to my ribs and all thoughts of lounging disappeared as my body was instantly converted to vertical.

Apparently my mother had her own image among her peers to be considered and that trumped mine.

Who Was
That Masked Man?

A fiery horse with the speed of light, a
cloud of dust and a hearty "Hi Yo
Silver!" The Lone Ranger. "Hi Yo
Silver, away!"

With his faithful Indian companion
Tonto, the daring and resourceful
masked rider of the plains, led the fight
for law and order in the early west.

Return with us now to those thrilling
days of yesteryear. The Lone Ranger
rides again!

During my childhood, the cowboy was king. This was the case in the movies, on radio, in books, in magazines and in comics. The Cisco Kid, Hopalong Cassidy, Gene Autry, Roy Rogers, Lash Larue and Mark Hatfield Texas Ranger, were all part of my life. Of all of these champions, none played a more prominent role than the greatest western hero of them all, the Lone Ranger!

Here was a person who embodied all the positive values of human kind. He fought against injustice without ever killing anyone or even hurting them badly. He was a champion of the poor and downtrodden, had a high respect for women, valued and befriended minorities, trod gently through the environment, was kind to animals and did all of this while keeping a clean and neat appearance. It was no wonder I loved everything about him and wanted to be like him. In fact for much of my childhood, I was him.

Countless hours of play time were spent acting out adventures in this persona. The haystacks became the hills through which I rode my fiery horse. The buildings on our farm became the towns which I rescued from the many villains that always plagued them. Sticks, both long and short, became weapons that I used to right the wrongs I encountered.

Just before supper with the chores finished, I would hurry into the house and turn on the radio in order to hear the latest adventure of the masked man and his faithful Indian companion. My breakfasts had to be General Mills Cheerio's because that's what was advertised during this program. At one point the Cheerio's boxes contained western figures that I faithfully collected and the boxes had building cut-outs that gradually became a western town. Why for a time I was even a card-carrying member of the Lone Ranger Health and Safety Club!

My life as the masked crusader was greatly enhanced one Christmas by the arrival of a fabulous gun and holster set. What a treasure! It was made of leather, had a ring of bullets held neatly in their loops around the belt which had a magnificent silver buckle on one end and a silver tip on the other. The holster itself had a silver star decorating its side. The gun was a cap pistol but was used without those accessories most of the time. It didn't really matter as I could make much more interesting gun sounds myself!

What a toy! It was probably the most used plaything any child ever received! Very soon I became the quick draw champion of my area of the Wild West. The lawless feared me even more now that I had this mighty weapon always at the ready. The hills resounded with even louder gunshots as I pursued these ruffians and put them out of business.

A more realistic gun with a revolving cylinder capable of holding a round paper with six caps on it eventually replaced the first gun. The holster was at one point cut down and the belt was lengthened to hang lower, both of which facilitated a quicker draw. There were no outlaws who could hope to be a match for such a well-equipped crusader for law and order.

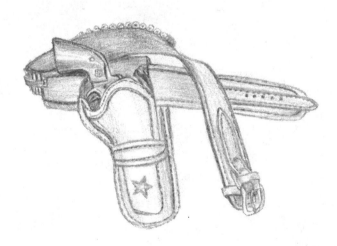

Throughout my childhood years, leading the fight for law and order in the role of the masked crusader was a regular occurrence and all the while the values promoted by this media character gradually became important considerations in my daily life.

Some years ago my wife and I attended a Halloween party dressed as The Lone Ranger and Tonto. We entered the gathering place to the strains of the William Tell overture and I experienced goose bumps as I was transported back to those thrilling days of yesteryear when the fight for law and order was black and white, justice was certain and swift and the heroes were flawless.

The Big Game Hunt

Stillness was the key. Breathing stopped as my finger tightened around the trigger. A satisfying snap and a powered missile launched itself toward the unsuspecting target. Any opportunity for evasive action evaporated as within a split second the jarring impact rendered the tin can ineffective for any further containment.

I don't recall how old I was when I was allowed to begin using a real rifle, but by the time I was a teenager I was what I considered to be an accomplished marksman. Mind you I had no one to compare myself to, except the Lone Ranger. I inherited a single-shot twenty-two that was scarred and weathered from years of use. It became my constant companion and a source of much enjoyment. I could now live out my cowboy fantasy in a much more realistic manner.

No tin can or discarded glass jar was safe. Occasionally sparrows were my targets but the greatest thrill of all was the big game hunt which took my attention every summer. The gopher population seemed to erupt like the green spring grass in the pastures. This wildlife was fair game for my assaults because it was seen to be a destroyer of crops and a general nuisance and danger because of the many burrows littering the fields.

The gopher was also a very worthy adversary since it tried to avoid my relentless pursuit, much like the villains in my earlier play. Marksmanship was in high demand since the size of the rodent precluded a careless shot in its general direction. Many times a shot from several yards away at a spot seemingly no larger than a silver dollar was required.

As I got older I devised alternative methods to deal with this foe. Sometimes I used a paperback book as a hunting accessory. I would move quite close to the target which would of course disappear, at which time I would sit down, set up my sniper position, pull out my book and read. Curiosity would eventually cause the target to reappear and seeing no threat in this lump that was just sitting there reading, it exposed enough of itself to come into line with my sniper's rifle.

In later years, farm work, much of it now on a tractor, took more of my time. Not to be deprived of my favorite pursuit, I devised a rifle scabbard which I attached to the tractor so that I could continue my hunting on tractor back. It wasn't quite the same as a fiery horse, but it worked quite well. The gophers were always very curious when they heard the motor noise and couldn't resist investigating. There weren't many circuits made on the field without the sound of gunshots.

Years later, a Christmas gift from my wife brought an Anschutz twenty-two repeating rifle with a scope and several clips for bullets. What a beauty! The stock was shiny and smooth, the hardware was well-oiled and unmarred and its accuracy potential was without equal. No longer would I have to lie in wait near the target since the scope would allow me to hunt from a greater distance. Unquestionably, no target, especially gophers would be safe from a person equipped with such a remarkable weapon.

Although I appreciated that gift, it was never used or enjoyed as much as I expected. The gopher population, it seems, no longer has anything to fear from me.

That's

Entertainment

Creative entertainment was only as far away as my mind, which was a good thing, since the opportunities to experience entertainment created by others was quite rare indeed.

One such rare occasion was the Wilf Carter concert that came to our town. I don't know what penance we had to go through to get permission to attend such an event but there we were. What a show it was! I wanted to be a performer from that time on. The fact that Wilf's two adolescent daughters were part of the show might have had something to do with it. To a young lad they were beautiful older women and I fell in love instantly. Their autographed family photo was a treasure that I would cherish my whole life, I was sure. With the passing of years, though, I lost track of the photo and of them, and sadly they made no effort to continue our special relationship either.

There was also the annual stampede, complete with parade, rodeo events and the most magical place on earth... the midway! It was a good thing I was given only one dollar to spend, because I would have fallen for every Carney pitch that was given. What wonders lay inside the tents where exotic people and creatures were pictorially represented! Was there really a man with two heads or a bearded lady? Given my limited funds, I had to choose my entertainment carefully. A midway ride or two was a must, of course. The salt and pepper shaker was thrilling beyond compare, or so I told everyone later.

During the ride I was mostly praying that it would stop before I threw up.

I did come away from the midway with a silver star on which I was able to have my name imprinted. It was a great addition to my lead role in the Lone Ranger sagas.

Out of the Chute

I was actually in a rodeo event one day... at least it had all the thrill and excitement of one! Together with my cousins, who were only slightly more daring than I, we made use of a corral full of yearling steers and held our own 'wild bull riding' event. Since no timer was present I don't know if the eight-second ride was ever achieved, but much effort toward that end was expended. Our backsides certainly felt the effects of this activity while with each spill another aromatic layer was added to our clothing.

By the time we went to the house for supper, our own fragrance left no doubt as to where we had been all afternoon. My uncle must surely have wondered why his steers were so skittish for the next few days.

There's A Love Knot in My Lariat

My rodeo skills were not limited to riding steers. I also became quite accomplished with the lariat. I practiced my roping skills diligently on every fence post in sight.

To make the activity more realistic I saddled up the corral rail and did my roping of the nearest posts from this mighty steed.

Having achieved the skill level of one catch in every ten throws I knew I was at last ready for the real thing, so I coiled my well-worn lariat and headed for the nearest animal herd. Being such a wise person, I figured I would start with something more my size and picked on a calf that was just a month or two old.

Snagging such an elusive prey would ordinarily have been no easy feat, but this creature was no match for my practiced throw. Sure enough the tenth one landed squarely around its neck. Wow, what a thrill! My practice had paid off!

It was then that I realized I had no idea whatsoever about the next step in this scenario. The *"Now what?"* had never occurred to me until the point when the animal darted off and the rope slipped from my clutches. After

much travail, I had to concede defeat. I could not catch the calf to remove the rope from its secure location around that animal's neck. I finally went to find my father who helped me with this most embarrassing task. I described to him how I had been innocently practicing roping fence posts and this calf just ran into the loop of my lariat. I was quite offended when he didn't believe me.

The Singing Cowboy

No self-respecting cowboy's life would be complete without a guitar. Gene Autry and Roy Rogers had seen to that while Wilf Carter made sure that the list of cowboy songs was long and varied. My older brother, while observing my many forays into the cowboy lifestyle, must have noticed the lack of the musical instrument as one day he presented me with a second-hand guitar that he had purchased for ten dollars.

Fortune had smiled in anticipation of this adventure because one of the song books in our house contained a page diagramming basic guitar chords. This page became my teacher as I doggedly labored to master the basic chord changes to accompany the various lyrics I had learned. Much of this early practice seemed to take place outside, probably due to the encouragement of those who didn't have an appreciation for 'well-played' country music. Sitting on the corral fence and serenading the animals that couldn't get away would have been the setting for my first performances.

47

Gradually the strumming sounds began to approach the tuneful stage and the chord changes became steadily smoother. Before long I was able to accompany my sister's piano playing and eventually joined the family Christmas instrumental ensemble. Although the ten-dollar instrument has long since been replaced by one of better quality, the guitar has been a source of personal enjoyment to this day.

Cowboy Heaven

The ultimate culmination of my life as a cowboy came during my early teens when one of our mares gave birth to a foal which somehow became mine. As it grew I read all that I could about training techniques and practiced them on this animal. "Dusty" became the actualization of the imaginary steeds of my childhood.

It seemed to me that I was bucked off more often than I climbed on as I gradually trained him for riding, but eventually he responded and I was then able to bring many of my previous fantasies into reality. Together with a neighbor boy who also owned a horse, we spent many afternoons riding the range enacting the cowboy tales of our youth.

Boy Against The Sea

An annual event that brought with it many opportunities for creative pursuits was the spring thaw. When the mounds of snow in and around the yard melted they produced rivers of all kinds to play in. Hours were spent launching mighty water craft to navigate these various tributaries. Rubber boots were often not tall enough as I would run beside these vessels on their journeys to the sea. This 'sea' was merely the largest body of water around, a slough by strict definition, but much more than that in my mind's eye.

This great body of water almost proved to be my demise. As the runoff collected on it the ice sagged in its middle, creating a pool of water surrounded by smooth, sloping gradients of ice. Gleefully following my ship on its final plunge into this mighty ocean, I suddenly realized that I had no traction and that I was sliding inexorably toward the center and into deep water. What to do? It was probably an instinct for survival that kicked in at the last moment. I dropped on all fours and with hands and knees apparently offering more traction than the bottoms of my rubber boots I was able to navigate my way up the slope to the shore. I came away from that experience with a new respect for my own limitations in contrast to even the gentlest forces of nature.

It Takes a Village

While waiting for my siblings to get home from school, I tried to invent new ways of filling those long hours. Even though there were lots of outlets for the imagination nearby, it seemed that the boundaries of our farmyard were too restricting for my inquisitive nature, so one afternoon I wandered up the lane to the road and requested a ride from a passing neighbor.

We drove to his farm where he lived with his mother and several siblings all much older than I. For the remainder of the afternoon I played in their yard and house. When suppertime came, I joined them for this event also. What wonderful treasures and comforts they had access to! Electric lights, indoor plumbing, an electric guitar and best of all... bicycles! Oh how I wanted such a conveyance!

Before long I was able to experience this ultimate method of transport. Apparently they decided I couldn't stay there forever, as two of them got on their bicycles, placed me on the handlebars of one, and took me home.

Not until years later did I wonder if my parents knew where I was during those hours. Did they miss me at all or were they glad someone else was entertaining me?

I Heard It on the Radio
Our strongest link to the outside world was a tube radio encased in a light brown wooden cabinet with beige cloth covering a speaker and two dark brown knobs for volume and tuning control. It was purchased at the local general store and installed in the bedroom that my brothers and I shared. A stack of two boxes served as a component

cabinet with the radio perched on top, its battery on the next level and various books and magazines in the lower one.

The most critical part of this 'component system' was the battery, a huge device, larger than the radio itself. It was attached to the radio by several wires which had to be aligned just so in order for current to be supplied properly. Station reception varied in direct proportion to the newness of this power supply and since a replacement was considered very expensive, rationing of listening time was often imposed.

The antenna on the radio traveled from the set through the wall and for about twenty feet along the fence outside the house. Although that may seem like a long antenna for such a small radio, its efficiency was remarkable. Stations from all over North America and occasionally beyond were frequently pulled in.

One such station, in the southern United States offered a weekly gospel music program which drew my brother's interest. As a regular listener he became aware of a special offer to purchase the song book that the featured artists used. When it came in the mail a few weeks later it proved to be a treasure trove of all the latest gospel music. It was this book that contained the guitar chords I was able to learn from later.

Besides the local news and weather, my parents also enjoyed German language programming, a feature which may have mitigated the lack of opportunity to communicate regularly in their native tongue.

We children, however, were more interested in the series programming that was available to us. The Lone Ranger, the Cisco Kid and Sergeant Preston of the Yukon were among the many daily or weekly stories that stirred our imaginations. And in the tradition of families everywhere we departed from our parents' musical tastes and became interested in the current music icons of the day as Wilf Carter, The Carter Family and Hank Snow filled the room with their lyrical musings on life.

Eventually we were no longer able to obtain the kind of battery the old radio required and its presence in our lives faded along with the last dying power supply.

No Frigate Like a Book

My love for novels originated somewhere in the mists at the dawn of my reading career. As soon as I could comprehend what I was reading, books were a magic medium that whisked me away from my surroundings to a world of adventures. Any spare moment would find me embroiled in the escapades of many different characters. Zane Grey and Franklin W. Dixon were among the authors I regularly enjoyed, all the more so because their works were numerous and easily obtainable.

Being able to purchase a book was a rare experience due to the cost factor, so public libraries were the main source for my insatiable desire for new reading material. Our school library, while well-intentioned, was quite limited in the variety of its offerings, so I turned to the largest public library in the province... the University of Alberta Extension Library.

This institution had a library lending system that was free of charge and available to any resident in the province of Alberta. Upon becoming a member, my interests were comprehensively detailed by means of a questionnaire that was part of the application process. From that time on a package of two books would arrive in the mail each month. When I was finished with them, I placed them back in their original packing envelope, turned the address card around in its slot and shipped it back to its source, postage prepaid.

Although in many cases the passage of time has removed the enjoyments of my youth, the current provincial library system has evolved to a similar standard of that time. From my home I can order a book from almost any public library in Alberta and have it delivered free of charge to my local library. So I continue to be transported to diverse worlds of adventure through this magical medium.

The Gumshoe

On my fifty-ninth birthday the phone rang. Although that in itself was not very surprising, the source of the call was. As my wife handed me the phone she remarked excitedly, "You'll never guess who this is!"

She was right. As I held the phone to my ear an unfamiliar voice said "This is your old pal Joe Hardy." I knew instantly who my long distance caller was although we had not been in close contact for almost forty-five years.

I interacted with and became good friends with many of my schoolmates but from grade one through high school I considered this person to be my best friend. While many experiences that we shared were memorable in themselves, none has remained in my memory as firmly as our common interest in the private detective world of Frank and Joe Hardy.

As we read of their adventures in such books as "The Tower Treasure" or "The Yellow Feather Mystery", we decided that we were destined to become the same kind of super sleuths. To that end we began playing the roles, practicing all the detective skills that were portrayed in the stories. We even involved a few other school mates from time to time in various supporting roles.

To further our education in this art, we began collecting as many of the books in the series as we could afford. Each birthday brought a different book as a gift, with care being taken not to duplicate any that were already in our possession. By the time we outgrew this phase, between the two of us we had most of the volumes that were available.

On one rare occasion when we were both in town on a Saturday evening, we sacrificed the usual movie event and decided to put into practice our 'shadowing' skills on the streets. We would pick out a stranger on the sidewalk and then follow that person unobtrusively as they went about their business. I can't imagine how inconspicuous two young boys in a small town could be, but we were sure we had not been spotted. Our father Fenton Hardy, himself a world-famous detective, would have been very proud, we were sure.

Time and career choices have separated Frank and Joe Hardy by at least one thousand miles and although neither one ever became a private detective, it appears that they will always be connected by the memory of a shared childhood interest.

In The Line of

Duty

Although the word 'chores' may not have been used on our farm, the concept was definitely there. These tasks began as soon as it was deemed one could handle any job, however small, that had to do with the running of the household or the various farming activities.

The Grain Auger

The earliest one I have a vivid memory of was a chore that was assigned because of my young age, and therefore, my small size.

At harvest time, the threshing machine was often pulled next to a granary so that the grain could flow directly from the machine into its storage location. Since the granary was rectangular and not round as today, the grain did not flow evenly into all the corners. When the grain level was close to the machine outflow spout, I was sent into the ever-decreasing space above the grain to distribute it to all the corners. This was accomplished by sweeping it with my hands and arms into the desired spaces.

I had many dark thoughts about being forgotten in that narrowing, claustrophobic space and eventually being buried alive but just at the right moment my father always appeared and rescued me.

Today one would shudder at the thought of this task being assigned to anyone, much less a child, but it seemed to be a good way to achieve the desired outcome. Surprisingly, I have never been claustrophobic and to my knowledge have never had any nightmares because of those events.

Perhaps it was as a result of this experience that as a teenager I actually envisioned a round storage facility with a cone shaped bottom ending in an auger that would eliminate any manual grain handling whatsoever. Imagine my surprise when years later someone else brought this idea to reality!

Flag Waving

My mother had some unique approaches to being a farm wife. While I noticed that many of our farming neighbors had meals brought out to them while they were working the land, this rarely happened in our operation. My mother insisted that her work time was as valuable as that of any of the males in the group which resulted in meals being served in the kitchen as usual. So even if one were working in the furthest field from the yard, this work had to cease and the trip to the house made if one wanted to eat.

Summoning the workers to dinner was a chore that fell to me before I was old enough to do much else. I was required to take a white towel, scale the corral fence and scramble onto the roof on the low side of the barn. Once there I navigated to the highest peak where I would wave the white flag until a corresponding wave came from the field worker whose stomach had likely already been sending messages that he should look in the direction of the signal source.

It was with some satisfaction that I not only contributed to the smooth operation of the farming activities but also to the women's liberation movement that my mother had initiated.

Horsing Around

Invaluable assets to our farm efforts were the teams of working horses that applied themselves to a number of tasks. Harnessing these huge animals for the job to be done was the work of a strong and tall person, so when I was young, this task was for my observation only. But size and strength were not as important when it came to unharnessing the animals at the end of the day.

During harvest, daylight had often faded by the time a halt to the labor was called and once again I was pressed into service. The tired and sweaty beasts were brought to the barn where it became my job to look after them. I would undo all the necessary clasps and buckles and then reach on my tiptoes or from a milk stool to the top of the harness, pull it down and off the horse and then struggle to lift it to its peg on the barn wall.

Having accomplished that, the next task was to take these horses, two at a time, to the watering hole for a drink. There I was, a small boy, walking along in the dark with a huge animal on either side of me, leading them to water. Neither I nor anyone else seemed to think this was remarkable.

Home Fries

A regular chore that fell to the children in our family was the spring yard cleanup. After collecting any large debris that always seemed to accumulate over the winter, we would start with rakes and forks at one end of the yard and work our way towards the middle. This would then be repeated from the other end.

By late afternoon we stood before a large pile of waste that was ready to be incinerated. Before lighting the flame we would toss several large potatoes into the pile. Some time later, when cleaning up the smoldering remains, we would rescue these potatoes, now thoroughly baked, break open the charred skins and spoon out the tasty interior. It was a treat that had motivated my efforts all day and now proved the hard labor worthwhile.

Tall *(and Wide)* **in the Saddle**

Potatoes were the staple of our diet since they were easy to grow, kept nicely over the winter and were useful in a variety of delicious recipes. And we grew lots of them.

This acre of crop had to be kept weed-free, however, and that chore often belonged to me, my father and our work horse named 'Champion.' Tall and wide were the words I used to describe him. I had to be lifted onto him and then apply Olympic gymnastic moves as I attempted to straddle that broad back.

He was hitched to a small, two foot cultivator that would be pulled between the rows of potatoes. My father guided the plow as I directed Champion along the rows. It was a pleasant way to spend a few hours.

A Long Drink of Water

With time I developed enough muscle to carry a pail of water and that meant the task of supplying the drinking and washing water was something I could now execute.

Our water came from a shallow well and by all accounts was some of the better tasting in the area. Its disadvantage lay in its location. This well was situated a few hundred yards from the house, thus necessitating many daily trips to replenish the half dozen receptacles. Several pails needed to be filled with drinking water and kept ready in the porch. A special container at one end of the stove needed constant replenishment to provide heated water for household use.

On my first attempts, one pail full was all I could manage and that only with several stops along the way to rest. Gradually, however, I was able to carry two at a time and eventually transport them the entire distance without a stop.

In The Cool of Evening

Being strong enough to lift some weight put me into line to help with the stooking of bundles during harvest time.

Mature grain was cut with a harvester called a binder. This machine gathered the grain into a bunch called a bundle which it then tied together with twine. These bundles collected on a carrier at the side of the binder and were dropped in orderly rows around the field. Manual labor was then required to set the bundles vertically, leaning against each other in a formation called a stook. This vertical placement would ensure

that the grain cured and dried properly in preparation for threshing. When a field was completely stooked, there were rows of bundled grain awaiting pickup by horse and wagon to be taken to the threshing location.

This stooking was usually done in the evening when it was cooler and other chores had been completed. Often my father and all available children would go out into a field together and work on this task. There was great satisfaction in surveying a completed field before hiking homeward in the dark.

Want Milk?

As I grew older, chores evolved into work as I took my place alongside my older siblings and my parents in the daily exercises of farm work. Milking cows by hand was a necessary skill that had to be mastered. The motivation was that the better the skill, the faster one would be finished with one's allotment of cows. Although I considered myself to be quite accomplished at this skill, I never matched the expertise attained by my father… or my mother for that matter.

The speed with which I accomplished this chore was hindered by the occasional need for some distraction from the repetitive nature of the task. Sometimes I couldn't resist the temptation to give the ever-present cats a few squirts of fresh milk. Whether my aim was always true or not, the resultant licking and washing of faces indicated great appreciation for my efforts.

The Laundromat

The 'equality of work' issue was never discussed in our family because whether you were male or female the chores knew no gender bias. One could be called upon at any time to help with farm work outside, or housework inside. Thus, helping to clean house, doing dishes and collecting laundry from the line were all activities that were completely gender neutral.

Laundry was a huge production and at some stages required more than one set of hands. Summer or winter, the day began with the securing of sufficient water to wash the several loads that had accumulated.

All the muscle previously developed could not get enough water to the house for this major event, so a larger container was necessary. Until the day the farmhouse was vacated for good, this container was a wooden barrel, placed on a stone boat (a sled about 4 x 6 feet in size) and pulled by a horse or in later years by a small tractor.

Getting the barrel from the well to the house without losing most of the water on the way was quite a trick. Since the ride was most often jerky and much splashing occurred, it could have been decided that the clothes worn by those riding on the stone boat had already been laundered.

In a winter with a sufficient supply of snow, this hauling of water was replaced by the collection of snow from the yard. Whether water or snow, this collected ingredient was placed in large canning boilers and set on the stove for heating.

Thankfully we had for our use an automated washing machine... automated in that it was powered by a gasoline engine and thus did not require manual labor to operate. Load after load was agitated to the extreme with conversation being of necessity postponed until later. It's hard to communicate when there is a gasoline motor running inside the house.

At least we were astute enough to vent the fumes outdoors. A custom-made hole had been carefully installed in the outside wall to accommodate the exhaust tube.

Another technological marvel was the attachment on the washer used to wring water out of the clothes. It was both useful and dangerous, however. Since I was big enough to be able to handle the wringing chore, I was put to work with this task, giving my mother time to prepare the next load. Occasionally I misjudged the distance to the wringing rollers resulting in bruised and sore, but water-free, hands. Thankfully the mechanism was equipped with a quick release lever that was easily activated.

The energy efficiency of the drying system has not been equaled by any invention to date. The clothes line was strung between several poles in the yard, placed there for that purpose. As the wringing of each load was completed, the entire assortment was carefully hung to allow the prairie breezes the opportunity to do their job. Of course there was often the unwelcome interference of the odd passerby that would stir up the dust on the road and cause much muttering on the part of my mother.

While rain was usually most welcome, its appearance during this drying time was not greeted with nearly as much cheer, as it meant a quick run to gather the half-dry garments before that ratio was suddenly changed. Usually such a quick appearance of a rain storm was accompanied by a frontal boundary of wind and dust, so speed was of the essence and all available hands were called into action during such an emergency. As much fun as doing laundry was, doing it a second time in the same day was not a pleasant option.

The amount of effort required to cleanse all clothing, bedding and towels was nearly doubled in the dead of winter. Although the washing procedure was fairly similar, the drying was not. Yes, all items were still hung outside, although I never did understand why, because at the end of the day they would be brought back in, frozen stiff and seemingly as wet as when they left the house in the first place.

A drying line was subsequently strung up throughout all the rooms in the house and these frozen ice packs would be bent into shape around it. As the steam began to rise from each item, the relative humidity, I was convinced, rose to above one hundred percent. I now understand why laundry day only occurred every two weeks or so and why certain articles of clothing were not changed as often as we now deem necessary.

A Penny for Your Peas

In our household assisting with the ever-present work load was not just a parental desire, it was an expectation that allowed no variation. There was no tolerance of an "I don't want to" attitude. The idea of paying the children to do chores was also a foreign concept. No pay was expected and none was offered... except when it came to shelling peas.

For some reason my mother deemed that chore to be worthy of payment. Pay was calculated on the basis of the size of container that the shelled peas occupied. A cereal bowl full of peas was valued at one penny whereas a mixing bowl full brought in a whole nickel!

While the nickel was the more sought after currency it soon became evident that the larger bowl did not fill up nearly as quickly as the smaller one. The fact that many of my shelled peas ended up in my mouth did not speed up the process either. After trying the larger bowl only once, I finally reasoned that making a small earning several times was preferable to possibly never realizing a nickel at all.

Cleanliness is Next to Sunday

Cleaning the house seemed to be an unending, thankless chore. No matter how hard we tried, within a day the outside debris insisted on taking residence inside once more. Nevertheless it was a task that had to be carried out each day. The daily routine was merely to sweep each room and perhaps to wash the entrance at certain muddy times, so that was relatively simple. However, the weekly Saturday effort was a concentrated crackdown that left no corner undisturbed.

The activity would begin with the usual sweeping routine but then quickly focused on more specific attention being given to the washing and rinsing of every square inch of floor space including under the beds. That having been completed, the round can of Johnson's wax was brought out, a worn-out sock swathed over one's hand and copious quantities spread as evenly as possible. The polishing routine which followed was often achieved through much play and merriment as old socks were pulled over ones feet and Olympic skating techniques employed to buff the wax to a shiny finish.

When the entire house was spotless, my younger sister and I would play under the table on the shiny, clean surface as the odor of the freshly applied wax was gradually replaced by the aromas of my mother's fresh baking.

It's Better with Butter
There's nothing like the taste of homemade butter on fresh homemade bread! I can almost detect that flavor as I smooth my store-bought spread onto my store-bought slice. My mind flashes back to a scene in my mother's kitchen where a gallon of cream that had been collected from several days of milking and had been cooling in the icehouse, was now carefully poured into the butter churn.

Ours was a relatively small churn that would produce about two or three pounds of butter at one time. This appliance was driven by a cranking mechanism that led to a set of paddles inside the glass container. The advantage of the glass was that one could see the butter gradually taking shape.

This 'producing' was definitely not an easy chore. It took a few hours of steady cranking to separate the thick cream into lumps of butter and thin buttermilk. That cranking power was supplied in turn by the hands of my siblings and me. We would set the churn on the table or on our lap, if we were strong enough to hold it there, and begin cranking.

I found various ways to amuse myself while this chore was being carried out. There could be singing, practicing Sunday school memory verses, reading a comic that lay beside me, or just listening to or participating in the conversation that was going on at the time.

Although one would practice ambidexterity during this chore, inevitably both hands would tire and the next shift worker would be called in. I wouldn't stray too far, though, as after some rest, my turn would certainly come again.

Gradually the consistency of the cream changed and small lumps began to form as the liquid became increasingly thinner. The lumps made the churning increasingly difficult, however and eventually my older siblings and finally my mother had to take over the last minutes of the task. I didn't run away to play at this time either as I too was awaiting the reward of task completion.

Finally the lumps in the jar became one and the paddles would turn no more. The lid was opened and the remaining liquid, now buttermilk, was poured into a container and if not consumed on the spot, saved for later use in baking. The lump of butter was salted, formed into smaller shapes and wrapped in wax paper for storage. One small morsel was granted for immediate use and that was eagerly spread onto a wedge of homemade bread and savored with sighs of contentment.

The enjoyment was probably as much the satisfaction of having been an integral part of a team where each person's work was a valued and necessary contribution to the finished product. But I didn't think about that at the time, I just enjoyed the fresh butter.

Separating the Men from the Boys

Cranking the butter churn was a good training ground for the technique required in the more difficult task of operating the cream separator. This appliance had a much larger crank that needed more muscle and in fact, more skill.

Milk acquired from our cows each morning and evening was brought into a building appropriately referred to as "the milk house". Here stood a contraption that had a large stainless steel bowl perched on its top. The bottom of this bowl ended in a spigot from which the milk flowed into a spinning dynamo that encased a stack of about thirty thin cone-shaped disks. From here two spouts directed their output towards separate containers. Almost unbelievably this machine extracted the cream, sending it out one of the spouts while dispensing the skimmed milk out of the other one.

This cream separator was, like the butter churn, powered by human hands. Unlike the churning, in this exercise a steady speed was necessary to make the separator work at its optimum level. Turn too slowly and the cream would be too thin, turn too quickly and it would be too thick. After some training and experience I could discern the correct speed just by the whine of the spinning machine.

Since the cranking task could not be abandoned until the entire milk harvest was put through the machine, at least one other person was needed to pour the remaining fresh milk into the top bowl and to replace the full receptacles of cream and skim milk as needed.

The resulting containers of cream were transported to the ice house where they were stored until used in food preparation or sold to the local creamery. The skimmed milk was distributed to the many hungry animals awaiting its arrival. Cats, pigs and calves were in turn nourished with this liquid.

For a few years after my older siblings set off on their own adventures, I was the main power behind the separator. Shortly before it would be my turn to also abandon the premises, we purchased an electric separator thus reducing the amount of person power required for the task.

And with that bit of progress the cranking chore faded into history.

It was neither the first nor the last time that a person would be replaced by a machine but in this case also, the human experience had lost another opportunity for collaborative interaction.

Getting There

Is

Half the Fun

The heavy rainfall warning bulletin echoes from the radio, but I pay it no heed as I start my truck and drive into the downpour. The wipers create a soothing cadence as I travel along the smooth asphalt to my destination one hundred kilometers away. Should the unlikely appearance of an impassable section of highway present itself, I will merely switch into four wheel drive and continue around it. Today I take such trouble-free travel for granted but it was not always so.

The possibility of motorized travel to and from our farmyard was strictly controlled by the vagrancies of the weather.

During the winter the largest snow drift in the area invariably decided to take up residence in front of our house, effectively blocking the lane that led to the road. For months this prevented any vehicle from leaving or entering the yard.

Throughout the summer any rainfall immediately turned the roads into vehicle-disabling mud and to attempt navigation was a futile exercise at best.

Many of my parents' grey hair likely resulted from the anxiety incurred when family members were expected to arrive for a visit and the roads were treacherous or impassable. The relief when their arrival was successful was always short-lived since before long it was replaced by the anxiety regarding their departure.

Even though tractor, truck and car did gradually make an appearance, no matter what challenge the weather presented, horses still provided the most reliable method of transportation.

Jingle Bells

During the long, cold winters the most common conveyance was an open sleigh that would seat at least six people and was pulled by a team of two horses. Throughout my first years of school, it was the primary means of getting us to and from that institution. To accommodate this mode of travel our school yard also included a stable, and it was here that the animals were boarded until it was time for the homeward journey.

One such trip was especially memorable in that it highlighted an advantage of that mode of transportation over any that have since been developed...the ultimate in remote control. During the afternoon of that day a blizzard came howling out of the north and all transportation by motorized vehicles ground to a halt. My brothers, however, hitched up the horses to our sleigh and piled blankets around and over all of us. The usual click of the tongue and snap of the reins gave the order for the animals to proceed. Without any further direction they took us across the fields to our farmyard and when we crawled out from under our warm coverings, we were home.

In my grade two year our whole family used this same sleigh to take us to the community hall for the annual evening school Christmas concert. On the way we were treated to an Imax spectacle as the darkness sported a clear sky replete with starry heavens that would have thrilled any astronomer. A plethora of sound effects accompanied us as we journeyed. The creak of the harness leather, the snorting of the horses and the squeak of the sled runners on the snow merged with snippets of conversation, creating the feeling that this must surely be the most perfect evening ever. On the journey homeward, these same sounds lulled me gently to sleep.

"Otto-mation"

The first motorized vehicle that my family owned after moving to our farm was a circa 1934 Ford car purchased from a neighbor. I expect that the main reason it came into our possession was its affordability. Age not withstanding, for some years it served to ferry us from place to place.

This automobile had a distinct advantage that suited the condition of the roads over which we traversed. Its chassis was quite a distance above the ground and so it could cross over some high protuberances without scraping or damaging its underside. A soft ride was not one of its strong features, though, since the navigation of one such rough spot created a heaving motion that caused even my mother's well-secured hat to become airborne.

A few years later my father bought a brand new one-ton truck and the old car lost its appeal for regular transportation. It did not lose its usefulness, however.

At various times, parts of the motor were removed and used in other applications. At one point the undercarriage, which included the frame and wheels, was detached and modified to become a wagon chassis. This frame was designed to hold various types of interchangeable, load-carrying containers such as a hayrack and a grain box.

Luckily for me, the body of the car and its interior remained intact, parked beside our vehicle garage, where it became various kinds of transportation in my play. From a thief's getaway vehicle to a winning racing machine, it never let me down.

While our new truck could not match the charm of its predecessor, it had its own attractive qualities. One that I particularly enjoyed was the open box. While all seven of us sat inside the cab on formal occasions such as the Sunday afternoon church jaunt, at other times adult comfort was the guiding principle, and several of the children made the journey sitting in the box.

Whether on cooler days, bundled up in blankets, or on warm ones we enjoyed the breezes and prairie scents as we traveled the dusty roads. On the night time return trips the heavens often provided an entertaining show for us. While we didn't have the planetarium commentary, the expanse and wonder of the starry array made its impression.

In the latter part of the decade my father bought a brand new 1957 Chevy, which although an unremarkable vehicle at the time has now become a car collector's favorite. Had I only known!

This was the vehicle in which I practiced parallel parking between two empty barrels, took my driver's exam, courted the girl that was to become my wife and drove my new bride to our first residence. It was also the car that I eventually sold for just ninety dollars.

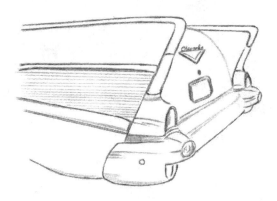

You've Got Mail

I walk into the air-conditioned foyer of the local post office digging in my pockets for the key to number 1034. I open the box and remove the usual assortment of flyers that beckon me to the city, a satellite TV bill, the local paper and a wedding invitation requesting a reply by email.

I nod a greeting to the other person also collecting his daily correspondence as I deposit the flyers in the recycling box and leave the building.

It was an ordinary trip to pick up the daily mail and I usually don't give it a second thought, but on this day I think about similar occasions several decades earlier.

Our little hamlet, which can't even be found on a map today, sported a general store and gas station, a grain elevator, a school, several residences and a post office. The latter was an unassuming building which most of the time leaned quietly against the breeze, but during two days of the week became the scene of a flurry of activity.

Although referred to as a post office, it was more of a shipping and receiving depot with mail being only a part of the exchange taking place. The local farmers brought their eggs and cream to this spot and left them for the mailman to transport to the creamery in town. The empties were brought back about a week later when they would be picked up by the owners and taken home. On occasion the mail truck also chauffeured a passenger who needed a ride into town on that day.

Since the arrival time of the truck varied, neighbors often began to drift in at least an hour early. Besides a stop at the general store for a few supplies, there was nothing left to do but loiter in the post office and exchange the latest news until the mailman arrived. Of course it was the perfect time to buy postage for the latest letter to be sent to the children in Calgary, the general contents of which would be shared as part of the local news. It wouldn't do to mail such a letter without explaining where it was going and what information it contained.

Once the mail delivery truck arrived it was still not possible to make a quick exit. The visiting just continued for awhile as the postmaster took the packages of mail and sorted them into boxes for each local resident. Finally when the sorting was completed, she would take a bundle from a box, call out the name of the person to whom it belonged and wait while he or she untangled themselves from the group to take it.

On occasion some good or even sad news brought by this bunch of mail had to be shared immediately thus spreading the joy or sharing the sorrow. When the grade nine departmental exam results were expected, parents waited nervously and in a more subdued manner until the envelopes were given to them. There was little privacy expected and perhaps none desired as sighs of relief or expressions of disappointment revealed the results.

Gradually as everyone received their items they would slowly drift away to their vehicles and return to the tasks that awaited them at home. It was a satisfying social time and as often as I could I would accompany my father or older sibling on these excursions.

During the school year, especially in the winter when roads were more difficult to negotiate, the school bus became an extension of the post office. Before going to the school at dismissal time the bus driver would drop by to check if any of the people on his route had not picked up their mail. If that was the case the postmaster would package those items inside the current issue of the Western Producer or Star Weekly and secure them tightly with string. Stacked by the bus driver's feet, they waited until the correct stop was reached whereupon they would be given to the disembarking child.

With the mail now safely at its destination my mother would listen to whatever community news we had brought and then immerse herself in the latest letter from her sister in Germany or the long-range weather forecast in the new issue of the Country Guide magazine.

O Christmas Tree

The arrival of a large, plainly wrapped parcel sent the clear message that it was almost time. The package was addressed to 'The Pahl Family' and it came all the way from the big city of Calgary. In it were several smaller packages in brightly colored holiday wrappings, each with a different family member's name written on it. It had been sent by my older brother, who although he would be coming home for Christmas, thought it important to send these expressions of affection in advance. Somehow it made his arrival all the more special when it did occur.

Of the many events that preceded Christmas at our house, the arrival of that package was one of the most special. Others came close. The school and church concerts with their small gifts and goody bags, the purchase of a tree on a Saturday trip to town, the smell of Christmas baking and the preparation of the annual fudge allotment were included in this number. Anticipation was high as the days were counted down.

Being a member of a large family revealed its greatest benefit during this holiday season. In addition to creating the requirement for more gift preparation and the secrets that needed to be kept as a result, there was also the anticipation of older siblings and their family members coming home to participate in the festivities.

Arrivals were always greeted with delight especially by a youngster who had no understanding of the logistics that were required to house and feed the number of people this represented.

Our living room, used only for special occasions such as when adult company was present, had been gradually transformed by the accoutrements associated with this magical time of year. A tree wearing festive ornaments adorned one corner. Under it many wrapped treasures mysteriously appeared during the final days before, the main event. The entire room waited in hushed silence for the cacophony of sounds that were about to be crammed into it.

The usual evening farm chores were no respecters of the season and on December 24th they seemed to take forever. But at long last all those present gathered round and without any master of ceremonies, began the traditional rhythm of activities that constituted our family Christmas celebration.

I learned one year what a high priority this family tradition had for my parents. Due to the variations of the yearly calendar, the church Christmas program had been scheduled for the evening of December 24th. Since the many children in our family occupied several key roles in this program, it was important that we be in attendance. However, since the date conflicted with our traditional family celebration, my father told the pastor that we would not be coming.

Shortly thereafter, we were notified that following much debate, a decision was made to change the date of the concert and our family tradition remained intact.

At least the first two hours of the evening were spent in caroling using a more or less equal mix of German and English Christmas favorites. The lyrics would be supported by musical instruments such as a pump organ (and in later years, a piano), a guitar, several harmonicas and an autoharp. Sprinkled throughout these sometimes less-than-harmonious renditions, were the recitations of the program items that had been learned for the school and church concerts. There was no rushing this part of the evening even though I wanted desperately to move on to the treasure-opening phase.

The 'program' always culminated in my Father's reading of the Bible Christmas story in the German language. To this day when I hear any scripture being read in that language, I could easily be persuaded that God's native tongue was German.

As I got older, the gift opening portion of the evening that had taken precedence in my childhood became essentially anti-climactic after experiencing the family harmony in the events that preceded it.

To Have and To Hold

Christmas celebrations are special in many ways. There is an abundance of savory treats of all kinds and my enjoyment is tempered only slightly by the warning given by my snug belt.

In my mother's house there was not nearly as much abundance, but what there was seemed very precious indeed and probably had to be rationed carefully among the many mouths that desired it. She had a unique way of doing this.

Each of her children had a similar sized shoe box assigned to them. It was filled with Christmas treats of all kinds: my favorite homemade fudge, a small assortment of store bought candies, nuts of various kinds, all still in their shells, some apples, a few Christmas oranges and homemade cookies.

When completed, the box was full and was presented to each child after the gifts had been opened. The rule was

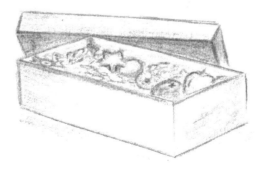

that the box of treats I received was mine and no one else could touch what was in it. I could enjoy its contents to my heart's content in any amount that I desired at any time. And oh boy, did I enjoy it!

The catch was that it had to last until New Year's Day, one week later, when it would be replenished for a final time.

Now I was not nearly as good at rationing as some of my siblings were. So when the favorites were gone and begging proved futile, I would have to take comfort in other pursuits such as walnut cracking contests where great pride could be taken by the person who had the hardest nut to crack.

When the refill day finally arrived, I could once more stuff myself. This time it didn't matter as much that my box was empty before the others' because by then the Christmas holidays were over and it was time for school!

The Department
of Education

Based entirely on hearsay, I decided that school was going to be fun. In fact I was so convinced of this that I left the security of the farmyard one day and set off on foot. I wasn't daunted by the fact that the school was several miles away or that no one accompanied me.

Although my intentions were good, I never did reach my destination. As my older siblings were already on their way home I encountered them about one third of my way there. Somehow they convinced me that I should join them on the trip homeward instead of continuing with my original objective.

With that plan thwarted, I just had to bide my time until I was of legal school age and could make the journey without being turned back.

A Star Is Born

My first day of school proved that hearsay had been right. What excitement and wonders were there to greet me! Unrestricted access to playmates; what could be more wonderful!

The older students, my brothers among them, saw to it that my first day was especially memorable. "Would you like to see stars through your coat sleeve?" they asked with obvious excitement in their voices. How could I say anything but an enthusiastic "Yes!" I never stopped to wonder why only my coat would do for this exciting activity, or how the stars could appear to me in the daytime. These were after all, experienced and learned men who had great wisdom to impart.

So, following the directions I was given, I lay down on the floor while they placed my coat on me and lifted one sleeve toward the sky. "You'll need to look very hard up the sleeve in order to see the stars," I was told. "If you don't have your eyes wide open, you may miss them." And as I gazed upward in wide-eyed awe, wondering when those stars would appear, they filled a cup with water and poured it down the sleeve. They had not been wrong. I did indeed see stars.

Play Ball!

My eagerness to please and to try anything once must have impressed these big boys, because later that same year I was asked to join their High School baseball team. Yes, that's right. I, a grade one student was asked to be on the big boy's team! Obviously they had somehow become aware of my baseball potential and wanted to capitalize on it.

I was placed in the enviable right field position and was certain that I could handle it as honorably as any major league player. The hitters on the opposing teams must have been aware of my skills as I don't recall them sending any hit out to where I was attentively watching the dandelions grow.

When our team was batting and before I was to step up to the plate for the first time, the coach instructed me to just stand there and not swing at any pitch. What kind of advice was that for such a power hitter, I wondered? I disregarded his directive and swung at the ball, sending it on a mighty arc all the way to the pitcher, who promptly caught it. It was an excellent way to discover the reasoning behind the coach's advice.

During the remaining opportunities to bat, my lack of height became the advantage the coach had foreseen, as almost every time I was able to secure a walk to first base. Once there, one of the older boys, a pinch runner I was told, would take over for me.

As an integral part of the team for the entire season, my pride knew no bounds as I surely must have been the envy of all my classmates.

Years later I found out that the real reason for my being there was two-fold: I was small, and therefore very hard to pitch to, but mainly I was young enough to bring the team's age average down to the required figure.

No matter. Baseball continued to be my favorite school sport, although subsequent years saw me among players my own age.

A Strapping Young Lad

No school memories would be complete without the recounting of a time when I earned the ultimate punishment. Usually I took great pains to be a model student and although I did like the resulting positive attention that behavior elicited from the teacher, I suspect it had more to do with not wanting my parents to become aware of any misdeeds.

Because perfection is elusive, I'm glad that I was protected by the prevailing wisdom of the day. If you misbehaved in school, you were punished in school... immediately. There was no need to consult with the parents on such matters. This was a very good principle as far as I was concerned since in my case double punishment for the offense would likely have been the result.

Being inventive and mechanically daring proved to be the ingredients for the first indiscretion for which I was apprehended. Several of us had devised some moderately powerful pea shooters out of clothes pins. They worked so well that we used them to ambush a trio of unsuspecting girls that happened to come into our line of fire. With unerring accuracy, all were subjected to some merciless target practice.

It never dawned on us that there might be consequences for this kind of action, but we soon learned about accountability. As our teacher applied several stinging whacks to each hand with a leather strap, we were convinced that we would do well to avoid future misdemeanors of this nature.

All the World's a Stage

It was rare that my parents took in school programs or performances. On one occasion, however, they were in the audience when I had the lead role in a school play.

I was cast in the role of 'Wildcat McGillicudy' who I understood was quite a mischievous character continually getting into trouble without trying very hard. How could any teacher ever think that role would be a good fit for me?

Actually, I had to audition for the part and achieved it only because I was able to do what the main character had to do repeatedly in the story... crow like a rooster. Since I could produce the most realistic sound on demand, I was chosen for the part.

In the plot, Wildcat unknowingly came into the presence of a hypnotist and was accidentally placed under a hypnotic spell. At the given suggestion of a certain word or sound, he would crow like a rooster and this at the most inappropriate moments such as when the pastor was invited to dinner.

Although I was quite proud of the role and did my best to

perform it with suitable enthusiasm, my father did not understand the plot and only saw his son making ridiculous crowing noises on the stage. As he sat in embarrassed silence with his head in his hands, I could imagine him thinking "For this I work so hard to send my child to school?"

Pot Bellies

Although I was born too late to be part of the one-room school era I experienced it in a small way during my eighth grade. At that time the Alberta Department of Education decided to spend taxpayers' money building new schools in many small communities in the province.

During this construction in our community an old one-room school building was moved onto our school yard and placed in a corner away from the building site. Luckily our grade seven and eight classes were assigned to spend a year in this building until the new edifice would be ready for occupancy.

Along with these rambunctious twelve to fourteen year olds bursting with newly released hormones, came an unsuspecting first year teacher, a young man of about twenty... a perfect recipe for a momentous school year.

This temporary school building came complete with a pot-bellied stove that was stoked with coal and wood during the heating season. Winter mornings found us with our desks crowded around that stove in an attempt to soak some warmth from its steaming efforts. As the day wore on we would gradually move further and further away to escape the rising temperature.

Moving a desk was an adventure in itself. Leave it to fourteen year old boys to discover unique ways of doing this. While the girls stood up and carefully pushed theirs into a new position, the boys would brace their feet on the floor, lift slightly and propel themselves 'Fred Flintstone style' along the scarred wooden floor. It was best, of course, to never move along the shortest route to one's destination.

Due to my inventive nature, I added an interesting mechanical device to my mobile workstation. An old alarm clock in our house was no longer keeping time, so my mother was going to discard it. I lay claim to it and through experimentation learned a technique that has worked well for me to this day; if something doesn't work, just take it apart, look at it and then reassemble it. Many times that will fix the problem. In the case of this clock, I was able to get the alarm part of it to work using this problem-solving technique.

I immediately recognized a brilliant educational application for this appliance. I cleared my desk of all unnecessary books and supplies, which then left it empty, placing them on a shelf in the room. I positioned the alarm clock, without its outside case, into the desk cavity so that the alarm hammer would strike the metal side when activated. The acoustic chamber provided by the storage cavity served to amplify the sound quite nicely and thus I had a warning system that I could use when my workstation was in motion.

My teacher was not nearly as excited about this creation as I was.

Prisoner of Love

A gymnasium did not appear in our small country school until after the construction of the new building was complete, so until that time almost all of our play was outside, no matter the weather. One of my favorite games, especially in Junior High was called "Prisoner's Base." In this game, two teams lined up on opposite sides of a marked area. Much running to and fro would occur as members of one team tried to tag the opposing players. When a tag was secured, the prisoner was placed in a holding cell at the opponents' end of the field. It was the duty of a fellow teammate to rescue this prisoner without being tagged in the process. If successful, the prisoner and rescuer had to run hand in hand back to their home base.

Besides being good exercise, this was the best way, and usually the only way, to not only get close to the girl of one's dreams but also to hold her hand for a brief but euphoric romantic interlude. Much thought and negotiation took place in advance of choosing teams so that the roster was exactly right for such liaisons.

Several such rescues of the object of my desire resulted in my gaining sufficient courage to ask her to dance with me at the next school dance. To my delight she agreed. Sadly, I knew even as I asked that I would never be allowed to go to such an event, and would have to disappoint her. I never did find out how she felt when the man of her dreams did not appear to whisk her onto the dance floor amidst the wonder, and the envy, of all the onlookers.

Happy Days

In a totally unexplained manner, in those Junior High years I came into possession of a black leather jacket. I gradually adorned this coat with silver buttons and stars in appropriate places. This was the ultimate style statement that only one other boy and I in that school were able to make. Long before I knew who "Fonzie" was, I had it seemed, impersonated the character.

This jacket was the only "chick magnet" that I ever possessed, and boy did it work. All the girls wanted to have a chance to wear it and how thrilling to bestow this honor on the girl of my choice on any given day. Whenever I was able, I would combine such a bequest with a stick of gum as well and the appreciation of the female was compounded accordingly.

WWF

Every child has heard stories from their parents of how teachers used to discipline students in "the old days". These story tellers of course also add the philosophical hypothesis that those discipline methods were somehow better than the ones employed in the present. My one experience with such a unique method would confirm that philosophy.

Two of the grade eight boys repeatedly did their best to provide a challenge to our young teacher. Although his long-suffering nature usually allowed these challenges to go by with only a reprimand, eventually his patience ran out and he took all of us outside where we formed a ring of spectators while he and the two boys squared off in a wrestling match.

To our surprise he was able to subdue both boys at the same time with seemingly little effort, holding each of their heads in an arm lock so they were unable to move. To my recollection they never gave him any further trouble. Of course, after that incident, the rest of us were also more reluctant to contest his authority.

Eventually our new school building was completed and with the advancement to grade nine, came a new teacher, a new building complete with a gymnasium and new pursuits to engage the imagination.

My one-room school days, regrettably, came to an end.

There's a Church
in the Valley

Since social interaction with other families was relatively rare, it was only natural that any chance to get together with my peers would be very significant to me. While my school experiences provided a great outlet for this need in my life, the other institution that facilitated this was the community church which we regularly attended.

The building itself came very close to the musical version of the "little brown church in the vale", except that it was white. It was an unimposing little building composed of a front porch and a main room, probably large enough to comfortably hold fifty to sixty people. It sat on a few acres of land otherwise occupied by wild prairie grass, a few graves, two outhouses and a coal shed. Inside it sported a pot-bellied stove, a few gas mantle lamps for use during the annual evening Christmas concert, some hanging curtain dividers to separate the various Sunday school classes and a collection of chairs and benches that accommodated the worshipping families.

Most days the main job of this building was to weather the elements but every Sunday afternoon it came alive with the sound of singing, laughing, praying and pastoral words of wisdom. For two hours people more or less forgot about their daily struggles to eke out a living from the unforgiving prairie, and gave consideration to more lofty concepts as they refined their own spiritual value system and hoped that their offspring would see its value as they did.

The building probably began to vibrate in anticipation the evening before, since that was the time to prepare for Sunday school. In many homes of the area the call "Have you done your lesson yet?" was to be heard, and children of all ages gathered by the nearest lamp with pencil, Bible and lesson book in hand to carry out this directive. The work, which I almost always enjoyed, involved reading the assigned text from the Bible and pondering appropriate answers to the questions in a small workbook provided for that purpose. The last step in this process was to memorize a related Bible verse for recitation the next day.

After lunch on Sunday, we would dress in our finest clothes, pack all seven family members into the cab of our one-ton truck, and drive the six miles to the church. Considering all the time that had been spent laundering, drying and ironing those nice clothes, it must have been somewhat dismaying for my mother to see how they looked by the end of that drive. I wouldn't be surprised if mini vans and crew cab trucks were the product of such a mother's frustrations!

My excitement grew as we pulled into the church parking lot and saw several vehicles already lined up and the neighborhood families entering the building. Inside, the seating always seemed to follow the same pattern. The children who were at least of school age sat in the front rows while the adults fanned out behind them. The elderly ladies, the group my mother was in, sat around the stove, which during the winter months afforded them the luxury of being in the only warm spot in the building.

A Happy Birthday to You

The meeting would begin with some singing, announcements and other rituals that were thought to apply to the whole group. One of these was the monthly birthday march. Everyone in the audience sang the religious version of the "Happy Birthday" song as those who had experienced this milestone during the past month marched to the front and deposited change of an amount equal to their age into an offering box. This money was then sent to various missionary causes around the world.

In our family, this tradition was carefully kept even though coming up with that amount of money for seven family members during the course of one year was a challenge. This was made even more difficult if there was more than one birthday in the same month as was the case with my father and me. It was a tribute to my mother that those amounts appeared in our hands on the appropriate day. Her only source of income was the payment we received upon selling our cream and eggs to the local creamery. These funds were then used to buy whatever groceries we couldn't produce on our own, as well as clothing, school supplies and many other miscellaneous items which included the church offering obligations.

106

The Meeting in the Car

After the conclusion of these 'opening exercises' everyone would divide into various age groups for the day's Sunday school classes. Now in a small building, there were only so many divisions that could be made, so some of these groups moved outside. When the weather was warm and sunny this meant a pleasant outdoor gathering in one spot or another. When it was not so warm, these outdoor gatherings moved into vehicles in the parking lot. As if my clothes hadn't already suffered enough, my age group was usually one that was 'pressed' into this kind of setting. In hindsight I have to admire the dedication of the instructors who shared those uncomfortable spaces with us time after time.

Summer School

My church social life also included a week-long summer event for children called Vacation Bible School. I eagerly took part in this opportunity to connect with my friends in what I viewed as a five-day party. Although each day consisted of several classes with Bible lessons, I never found it onerous because not only did I enjoy the stories and the singing, it provided a much-needed time of interaction with my friends in the middle of two months of school holidays with their forced social separations.

And then there were always the breaks, just like at school. Recess and lunch would find us playing various games that used up some of our stored energy. 'Flying

Dutchman' was one of my favorites since it involved holding hands with girls. The game itself was a version of tag that started with one couple being 'it'. The remaining players stood in a circle holding hands. The 'it' couple ran around the group and tagged another couple in the circle by touching their joined hands. The tagged couple then left the circle and raced around in the opposite direction in an attempt to rejoin the circle at their original position before the 'it' players reached that spot. Either way, if I was holding hands with the current object of my desire, I was a winner.

All Day Sing and Dinner on the Ground
The annual church picnic was another highlight for this socially starved youngster. It was held in a treed, outdoor location, although finding such a spot in the Alberta Special Areas region must have been a challenge.

The afternoon would consist of novelty races and ball games, both of which were exactly up my alley. Even with my leg tied to that of another runner or when bound inside a burlap sack, I felt myself to be fleet of foot and equal to the challenge. It didn't matter whether I came in first or not. After all, since God was no respecter of persons, rewards were given to every participant that day.

The celebrations would last into the evening hours and usually culminated in a roaring campfire with participants sitting around it singing and visiting. The group of youngsters, of whom I was always an enthusiastic member, would use the fading daylight as an opportunity to play hide and seek among the trees and cars. There was no lack of physical activity that day and it was not uncommon that by the time families packed up to leave for home, many of us had to be carried to our vehicles.

For We Have Seen His Star

Near the end of December the little church building would experience its only evening event of the entire year. The gas lanterns with their glowing mantles hissed incessantly while the pot-bellied stove offered what warmth it could to its surroundings. A Christmas tree adorned one corner of the stage and the minister's pulpit was moved to the side so that all presentations could be seen clearly. It was time for the annual church Christmas program.

The evening would find the little building bursting at the seams with standing room only that spread into the porch and even outside. It was the one event of the year when everyone in the community found time to go to church.

Preparation for this occasion had begun weeks before, starting in the small Sunday school classes where each of us was assigned various parts in the program. These could range from individual recitations to group plays, depending on age, ability and somewhat less, on talent. It seemed that there was an essential role for everyone and these roles were treated very seriously.

Preparation then continued in the homes with mothers encouraging their children and listening to their ever improving attempts at mastery of the assigned role. My own mother knew every one of our parts from memory often before her children did. Performance time would find her mouthing them silently, or occasionally prompting audibly, while her children in turn carried out their roles.

Since ours was the only family in the church wherein the children could speak German, we were always given the additional task of preparing a German poem to recite for the audience, many of whom understood the language. My mother was a quiet, modest woman, but even as a child I could sense her pride when on the evening of the concert, her children would not only take part in all the English events, but would also contribute the only German ones on the program.

At the conclusion of the lengthy affair all the children were the gleeful recipients of small bags of treats. Nuts, candy and Christmas oranges filled the lunch-sized paper bags which were given the same respect as a pirate's treasure chest. It was, after all, a sign that we had done a good job and deserved recognition. The adults too, were able to take an orange from the boxes that were passed around like offering plates. I positively glowed with satisfaction as we made our way home following this superb occasion.

And It Came To Pass

Today all that remains of that church location are three concrete steps that lead up to a non-existent porch, the few graves on the property and the winds that still rustle the prairie grass.

Far more lasting have been the effects of the interactions that took place there. Character was instilled and reinforced. People were encouraged to aspire to higher ideals. Lessons of sacrifice and respect were taught and learned. Friendships were begun, continued and cemented. Children were allowed to be children and at the same time encouraged to grow up straight and tall.

And perhaps most importantly, God still seems a little more real and personal because of what I experienced in that place.

The

Mark

When I was young, I wanted to make my mark on the world so that in years to come, everyone would know I had been here. To accomplish that, I climbed a tree.

Outside the front door of our house was a large tree. At least it seemed huge to me. Many enjoyable hours were spent scaling this edifice as it became at different times a mountain, a rocky cliff, a skyscraper, a sniper's perch or just a tree. Seeing how high I could climb into its ever thinner branches was always a challenge.

It was on one of these climbs that I undertook to leave my mark on this planet. Trees live forever, I reasoned, and began to carve my name into its substantial trunk. A half-hour's careful work and with that, my place in history was forever assured. Succeeding ascents to its lofty heights made me confident that my mark was safe for subsequent generations to view.

As time and weather took their toll, the mark I had made on that farmyard slowly disappeared and today can no longer be found. Much more lasting, however, have been the marks that my experiences on that farmyard and in that rural farming community left on me.

Imprinted were all the positive values of human kind, which far from being an endangered species during that time, were exemplified in and by the variety of people I encountered, my family members included.

Working hard and cooperatively, being accountable for ones actions, deploring injustice, avoiding the negative while accentuating the positive, being sensitive to the less fortunate, having a genuine respect for the feminine gender, valuing minorities, treading as gently as possible through the environment, respecting the role of animals in our world and attempting all of this while keeping a clean and neat appearance are marks that influence me to this day.

The Lone Ranger would be pleased.

ABOUT THE AUTHOR

Otto Pahl is a man with not enough time.

As you can tell from his stories, boredom has never been an issue, and even now there is a long list of things that he would like to be learning and doing.

Throughout his adult life he has enjoyed reading, photography, playing the guitar, singing, backpacking, cycling, hiking, cross-country skiing and camping. For many years he was also a member of a music group that performed throughout western Canada.

Interactions with family and friends have always provided a source of pleasure for him and now that he has grandchildren, his childhood adventures can be relived once more. He can be found with them at various times going down a waterslide, giving 'under-ducks' on the swings, riding bikes to the 'secret fort', having water fights, coloring a picture or dressing up in various costumes as the different stories unfold.

While spending over thirty years as an educator in the Alberta school system he was also involved in many extra-curricular pursuits with his students and colleagues. He is now enjoying a variety of retirement activities which include a part-time job as a program coordinator at Olds College in Alberta.

He lives with his wife Karen on the sunny side of a quiet street in Three Hills, Alberta.

To obtain copies of this book contact:

OK Enterprises
Box 1034
Three Hills, AB
T0M 2A0

Or by email:

ok@kneehill.com